EQAO Grade 6 Language Test Prep

—— Teacher Guide ——

Written by Ruth Solski

RUTH SOLSKI was an educator for 30 years. She has written many educational resources and is the founder of S&S Learning Materials. As a writer, her main goal is to provide teachers with a useful tool that they can implement in their classrooms to bring the joy of learning to children.

Published in Canada by:
On The Mark Press
15 Dairy Avenue, Napanee, Ontario, K7R 1M4
www.onthemarkpress.com

Funded by the
Government
of Canada

Table of Contents

About This Book

This book was created to help Grade 6 students prepare for the EQAO Language Assessment test. The 10 tests have been designed to be very similar to the actual test the students will be taking. Many of the questions are asked in a similar way so that students can get familiar with the questioning format. Students will encounter different types of reading experiences as they make their way through the various tests including fiction and nonfiction stories, a newspaper article, a friendly letter, poetry, and informational text. They will then be asked to answer corresponding multiple choice and open response questions.

There is also plenty of writing practice as students are asked to write sentences, paragraphs, short stories, instructions, a description, a movie review, a poem, a letter and a newspaper article. There are also multiple choice questions featuring essential grammar and writing skills.

There is no particular sequence to the tests. They can be used in whatever order you choose to fit your students needs.

SSG114   ISBN: 9781487704032 © On The Mark Press

The Hired Hand

Brady didn't mind living with his grandparents except for one thing – Grandpa wouldn't let him have a dog. He'd coaxed and pleaded until his grandma said, "Listen, Brady, you'd better drop the matter because your grandfather's mind is made up."

1

"But why does he hate dogs so much?" asked Brady. "He's a farmer."

2

"Brady, it's important to your grandfather that all of our farm animals have a purpose. He thinks pets are just a waste of his hard-earned money."

3

One hot summer afternoon a couple of weeks later, just when Brady was beginning to think that getting a dog was an absolute pipe dream, someone dropped a dog off at the end of their road. Then the car roared away in a cloud of dust.

4

Brady couldn't believe it! The medium-size dog was tan-coloured, with bowed legs, a long, square head, and a tuft of whiskers hanging from its chin.

5

A terrier! For months Brady had been reading about different breeds of dogs and studying their pictures. He knew that terriers tended to be hyper and yappy. But this particular one just sat there in the middle of the driveway looking up at him with the most curious expression.

6

As Brady approached the dog, it cocked its head to one side, eyeing him curiously. Brady checked for a collar. There was none.

7

"What am I going to do with you?" he asked sadly. "Grandpa will never let me keep you, yet you seem like such a nice dog."

8

Brady hesitated, and thought for a moment. "Well we might as well go and face the music." He turned and started up the driveway. The dog immediately trotted along behind him.

9

"You sure are good-natured," Brady admitted. "Not as yappy and hyper as the books say your breed is."

10

SSG114   ISBN: 9781487704032 © On The Mark Press

At the farmhouse Brady left the dog in the yard and found his grandmother at the kitchen counter making bread.   11

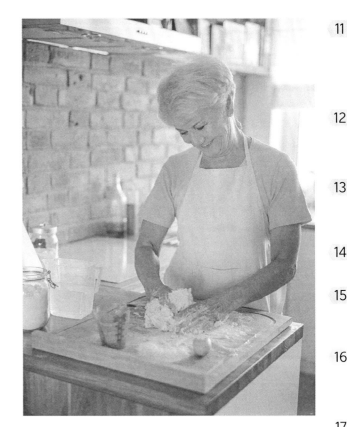

"Grandma, somebody dropped a dog off at the end of the driveway."   12

His grandmother nodded. "I saw you bring him up here. What kind is it?"   13

"A terrier mix, by the look of it."   14

Grandma kept kneading the dough. "What do you know about terriers?"   15

Brady hesitated. "They're inclined to be a bit yappy," he admitted.   16

"Not exactly an endearing characteristic."   17

"I know!" said Brady. "Grandpa doesn't even like good, quiet dogs."   18

The older woman looked up from her work. "That's not the point, Brady. I doubt if it'd make any difference to your grandfather how good-natured a dog is. He's only interested in having them earn their keep."   19

"Too bad we don't have any sheep. I could train him to be a sheep dog."   20

"Dogs were bred to be the way they are for particular reasons. Why don't you do a little research and see what you come up with?"   21

Brady frowned thoughtfully. What was his grandmother trying to tell him? With a puzzled frown he ran up to his room, retrieved several of his dog books, then returned to the yard. The dog was waiting patiently by the rose bush.   22

Brady dropped to the ground and opened the first book to the section on terriers. Cairn terriers, Jack Russells, Scotties . . . with each breed Brady would turn to the dog beside him and compare him to the accompanying photograph.   23

"I think you look most like the Irish Terrier," he finally said. The dog wagged his tail.   24

SSG114   ISBN: 9781487704032 © On The Mark Press

"Now what does it say about the Irish Terrier? Wiry coats, little tolerance of other animals . . . hmmm." 25

He looked again at the dog. "You seem to be a very tolerant fellow." 26

Bred to hunt and kill vermin. Brady's ears perked up. Irish Terriers are especially good at bringing to ground: rats, mice, and even foxes and weasels. 27

That was it! Now he knew what his grandmother had been trying to tell him. Their henhouse was so old it was becoming difficult to keep predators out – and there was no money to build a new one. Just the other day, his grandfather had complained about a weasel killing a couple of his chickens. And this past spring, a fox had killed over a dozen hens in less than 15 minutes . . . 28

Brady scrambled to his feet and raced to the kitchen. 29

"Grandma, I've go it! The dog can earn his keep by guarding the henhouse against weasels and foxes. Terriers were bred to kill vermin." 30

"So they were," his grandmother said with a faint smile. "When I was a little girl my father kept a terrier for that very purpose. I was hoping you would find out for yourself – and with a little research, you did" 31

"Thanks, Grandma," Brady said with a big grin. "Now we just have to convince Grandpa to keep him." 32

"Oh, I think that will be up to the dog. If he turns out to be a good guard dog, he'll be worth his weight in gold. If not . . ." she paused and smiled. "If our little friend has found a home here, what are you going to call him?" 33

Brady thought for a minute. "I'm going to call him Handy – short for Hired Hand," he said. "Just to remind Grandpa that this is one dog who will be out there everyday, protecting our chickens and earning his keep!" 34

The Hired Hand: Questions

1. Why won't Brady's grandfather let him have a dog?

   ○ He hates dogs.

   ○ He is allergic to dogs.

   ○ He thinks dogs are a waste of his hard-earned money.

   ○ He thinks dogs are lazy.

2. Which of the following is the best definition of a "pipe dream" (paragraph 4)?

   ○ a dream about pipes

   ○ an unattainable or fanciful hope or scheme

   ○ something that is easy to come by

   ○ a dream about not getting a dog

3. From studying about dogs, what does Brady know about terriers?

   ○ that they are brown with bowed legs

   ○ that they are calm and friendly

   ○ that they do not get along well with other dogs

   ○ that they tend to be hyper and yappy

4. What does Grandma suggest to Brady in paragraph 21?

   ○ She suggests that Brady train the dog to be a sheep dog.

   ○ She suggests that Brady should do a little research.

   ○ She suggests that Brady talk to his grandfather about the dog.

   ○ She suggests that Brady should get rid of the dog.

SSG114   ISBN: 9781487704032 © On The Mark Press

The Hired Hand: Questions

5. Which of the following descriptions best describes the dog's temperament?

   ○ nervous and anxious

   ○ excitable and yappy

   ○ afraid and shy

   ○ good-natured and friendly

6. What kind of terrier does Brady think the dog is?

   ○ Cairn terrier

   ○ Jack Russell terrier

   ○ Irish terrier

   ○ Scottish terrier

7. What does the word "vermin" mean as it's used in paragraph 27?

   ○ poisonous plants that make people sick

   ○ small animals that cause trouble or harm to people

   ○ large animals that cause trouble or harm to people

   ○ small animals that are friendly and helpful to people

8. What is Grandma's attitude towards the dog?

   ○ She wants to help Brady find a way to keep him.

   ○ She doesn't like the dog.

   ○ She thinks the dog cannot be trained.

   ○ She thinks he is the wrong kind of dog.

9. What does the dog have to learn to do to have any chance of staying?

   ○ not bark very much

   ○ be a good companion for Brady

   ○ be a good guard dog and protect the chickens

   ○ be friendly to Grandpa

The Hired Hand: Questions

10. Explain why the chickens on the farm needed to be protected. Use details from the text to support your answer.

_____

_____

_____

_____

_____

_____

_____

_____

_____

11. Do you think Grandpa will end up letting Brady keep the dog? Use details from the text and your own ideas to explain why or why not.

_____

_____

_____

_____

_____

_____

_____

_____

_____

_____

_____

_____

SSG114   ISBN: 9781487704032 © On The Mark Press

Writing a Short Story

12. Write a short story about a pet that you would like to have that your parents may not approve of. Make a case for getting your pet.

   Ideas for my Story

_____

_____

_____

_____

_____

_____

_____

_____

_____

_____

_____

_____

* Remember to check your spelling, grammar, and punctuation.

This page will not be scored.

Writing a Short Story

Write your short story here.

_____

_____

_____

_____

_____

_____

_____

_____

_____

_____

_____

_____

_____

_____

_____

_____

_____

_____

_____

_____

_____

_____

_____

SSG114   ISBN: 9781487704032 © On The Mark Press

A Friendly Letter

2002 Summerhill,
Ottawa, Ontario,
H2H 1E3

February 7, 2016

Hi Carolina!

Melanie, here. I'm writing to you because I really need your help! I'll tell you about my love life later. First I should explain.

Our geography teacher assigned a huge project on the continent of our choice. The whole class is divided into groups; our group chose the Americas. Paul is going to do the history. Marie-Claire is covering geography. I get to do the economy. Yes, that's right, the economy of the Americas, but it does not include Canada or the United States. That means Mexico, Central America, and South America.

I've read quite a bit, but it's complicated. That's why I really need you to help me. You've been living in Lima for a year now, so you must know a bit about the region. Plus, you're a whiz at economics and math. Remember your scores in grade 4? And no wonder! Like father, like daughter. Your dad is working as an economist down there right now, isn't he? Maybe you could ask him. I also thought that since it's summer in Peru you'd be on holidays and have some spare time to help me out. So how about it, eh? How could you refuse your best friend?

Bye for now,

Melanie

P.S. I have to present this on March 27, so please hurry! I've enclosed a small bribe of two CDs, great new music that you'd be missing if it weren't for me.

P.P.S. Oh yeah, I broke up with Freddy!!!

A Friendly Letter: Questions

1. Why is Melanie writing her friend Carolina a letter?

   ○ to tell her about her about her love life

   ○ to ask for her help on a project

   ○ to see how she likes living abroad

   ○ because she is her best friend

2. Where does Carolina live?

   ○ She lives in Ontario.

   ○ She lives in Mexico.

   ○ She lives in the United States.

   ○ She lives in Peru.

3. Which subject is Melanie covering for the assignment?

   ○ the economy of the Americas

   ○ the history of the Americas

   ○ the geography of the Americas

   ○ the social life of the Americas

4. What time of year is it where Carolina lives?

   ○ Winter

   ○ Spring

   ○ Summer

   ○ Fall

5. About how much time is there between when Melanie wrote her letter and when she needs a reply?

   ○ about 3 months

   ○ about 7 weeks

   ○ about 2 weeks

   ○ about 10 weeks

6. What does the word "economy" mean as it is used in this letter?

   ○ the careful use of money

   ○ the cheapest way to buy something

   ○ the cheapest way to fly

   ○ the way a country produces, distributes, and uses its money

SSG114   ISBN: 9781487704032 © On The Mark Press

A Friendly Letter: Questions

7. Explain why it is a good idea for Melanie to ask Carolina for help. Use details from the text to support your answer.

_____

_____

_____

_____

_____

_____

_____

_____

8. Why do you think Melanie uses so many exclamation marks in her letter? Use details from the text and your own ideas to support your answer.

_____

_____

_____

_____

_____

_____

_____

_____

Writing A Friendly Letter

9. Write a letter to a friend asking for help with a problem. Make sure to include information about the problem and why your friend would be a good person to help. Remember to use the format for a friendly letter.

Ideas for My Letter

_____

_____

_____

_____

_____

_____

_____

_____

_____

_____

* Remember to check your spelling, grammar, and punctuation.

This page will not be scored.

SSG114   ISBN: 9781487704032 © On The Mark Press

Writing A Friendly Letter

Write your letter here.

Writing Multiple Choice

10. Read the following sentence. Which word or phrase is the best synonym for the underlined word?

He got lost in the <u>labyrinth</u>.

- ○ dense forest
- ○ underground mall
- ○ maze
- ○ tower

11. Which of the following words is best suited to complete the sentence below?

That puppy is _____ than I am.

- ○ quick
- ○ quicker
- ○ quickest
- ○ quickly

12. Which word is "mo." an abbreviation for?

- ○ month
- ○ money
- ○ Montana
- ○ many

13. The word "basketball" is a

- ○ predicate nominative
- ○ adjective
- ○ compound noun
- ○ proper noun

14. Which phrase is the correct ending for the following analogy?

Squirrel is to *nuts* as

- ○ worms are to robins
- ○ bees are to honey
- ○ robin is to nest
- ○ hives are to bees

SSG114 ISBN: 9781487704032 © On The Mark Press

Writing Multiple Choice

15. Which part of speech identifies the underlined word in the following sentence?

    The storm moved <u>quickly</u> over the lake.

    ○ adverb

    ○ noun

    ○ adjective

    ○ verb

16. Carefully read the following sentences. Choose the word that best completes the second sentence.

    Every Monday, Tuesday, and Thursday, Andy went to the library. He took _____ in speed reading.

    ○ machines

    ○ teachers

    ○ lessons

    ○ books

17. Which of the following is the abbreviation for "building"?

    ○ bg.

    ○ bldg.

    ○ bdg.

    ○ bld.

18. Which part of speech identifies the underlined phrase in the following sentence?

    The letter <u>on the desk</u> is mine.

    ○ verb phrase

    ○ noun phrase

    ○ adjective phrase

    ○ prepositional phrase

19. Which of the following words has the same meaning as "awe"?

    ○ curiosity

    ○ amazement

    ○ groups

    ○ awareness

Dealing with Failure

Sometimes life seems very hard and unfair, doesn't it? It is easy to get discouraged when things don't seem to go your way. You may even wonder if someone like yourself could ever be successful in life. Well, you can!

1

Years ago a young boy was born into a very poor family. The boy's parents eked out a living as poor farmers for many years, but in order to survive he had to help his family by working long, hard hours doing the farm chores.

2

When he was seven years old, he and his family left their home and all of his friends and moved far away to where his father had bought some new farm land. Only two years after their move, tragedy visited the small household. The boy's mother got very sick and died – an event that left a great mark on him for the rest of his life. He was only nine years old.

3

Like many children of his time, the boy did not have the opportunity to attend school regularly. But he was determined to learn to read and write – and he did – spending long hours practicing and improving his skills.

4

He left home at a young age and got a job as a store clerk, but lost his position a year later when the business failed. Later, he was appointed postmaster of his township and ended up having the worst efficiency record in the county. Not a good start in the work force, was it?

5

As a young man, he fell in love with a woman named Ann Rutledge. Her sudden death sent him into a terrible depression. It was during this unsettling time in his life that he developed an interest in politics and decided to run for the state legislature. You can imagine his disappointment when he lost – placing eighth among 13 candidates.

6

Although all of these early setbacks must have been terribly discouraging, they were not enough to keep this determined young man from pursuing his dreams.

7

SSG114   ISBN: 9781487704032 © On The Mark Press

Eventually, he did succeed in winning a seat in the state legislature and continued to gain the respect and admiration of everyone who knew him. Even as he became more successful as a lawyer and politician, he experienced great tragedy. His son died at the age of four, and he failed to be elected to both the senate and the vice presidency.

8

Finally, in 1860, he ran for the presidency of the United States of America. Not only did he win the election, he went on to become one of the greatest leaders in his country's history. The man's name was Abraham Lincoln.

9

Imagine if Abraham Lincoln had let his early failures and discouragements defeat him. Imagine if this great man had just given up and decided the he wasn't good enough – or that he didn't have anything to offer. Americans wouldn't have had this wise and gracious man's leadership through the darkest years of their history – the great Civil War.

10

Lincoln is an inspiring example of someone who faced great tragedy, failure, and disappointment and continued to persevere until he realized his greatest dream, and made a difference in the world around him. Looking back at the great trials that

11

Lincoln went through as a boy and as a young man, we can now see how this period prepared him for the even greater hardships he would face as president.

In the middle of the terrible Civil War, Lincoln did a remarkable thing. He issued the following proclamation to the American people:

12

"It seemed to me fit and proper that (the gifts of God) should be solemnly, reverently, and gratefully acknowledged with one heart and one voice by the whole American people. I do, therefore, invite my fellow citizens . . . to set apart and observe the last Thursday of November next as a day of thanksgiving and praise to our benevolent Father who dwelleth in the heavens."

13

Abraham Lincoln was an exceptional man, who despite a life filled with trials, as well as tremendous accomplishment, found that there is much to be thankful for.

14

Dealing with Failure: Questions

1. What does the phrase "eked out a living" mean as it is used in paragraph 2?

   - ○ make do with what you have
   - ○ make up for a loss
   - ○ get something with great difficulty
   - ○ make something last for a long time

2. What significant thing happened in the boy's life when he was nine?

   - ○ his mother got very sick and died
   - ○ his family left their home
   - ○ he moved far away from his friends
   - ○ he worked long hours doing farm chores

3. Why is paragraph 5 important to the story?

   - ○ It tells about him leaving home.
   - ○ It tells about his first failures.
   - ○ It tells about him being a postmaster.
   - ○ It tells about his childhood.

4. What do paragraphs 6 and 7 tell about the young man's character?

   - ○ He was an unsettled person.
   - ○ He was crippled by depression.
   - ○ He was not a very good politician.
   - ○ He did not let setbacks keep him from pursuing his dream.

SSG114   ISBN: 9781487704032 © On The Mark Press

Dealing with Failure: Questions

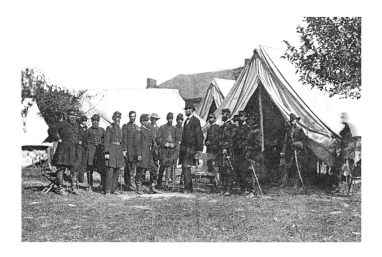

5. What tragedy occurred as the young man became a successful lawyer and finally got elected to the state legislature?

   ○ He became sick and almost died.

   ○ His son died at the age of four.

   ○ He and his wife got a divorce.

   ○ His business suddenly failed.

6. What does "the darkest years of their history" refer to in paragraph 10?

   ○ Lincoln's early failures

   ○ the terrible poverty of the time

   ○ the American Civil War

   ○ a time when everyone gave up

7. How did the events in Lincoln's early life prepare him for the challenges he would face as the president of the United States?

   ○ It prepared him to deal with the members of congress.

   ○ It prepared him to deal successfully with hardship and adversity.

   ○ It prepared him to deal with the soldiers in the war.

   ○ It prepared him to be strict when he had to be.

8. What remarkable thing did Lincoln do in the middle of the Civil War?

   ○ He became president of the United States.

   ○ He realized his greatest dream.

   ○ He set aside a day for the American people to give thanks together.

   ○ He briefly stopped the war to give the soldiers a rest.

Dealing with Failure: Questions

9. Why was Abraham Lincoln an inspiring man? Use specific details from the story and your own ideas to support your answer.

_____

_____

_____

_____

_____

_____

_____

_____

_____

_____

10. What do you think is the moral of this story. Use specific details from the story and your own ideas to support your answer.

_____

_____

_____

_____

_____

_____

_____

_____

_____

_____

SSG114   ISBN: 9781487704032 © On The Mark Press

Writing an Article

11. You are a journalist for the local paper. Write an article about an inspiring person. It can be someone you know – a teacher, friend or relative – or a famous sports figure, celebrity, politician, scientist or a historical figure.

Ideas for my Article

_____

_____

_____

_____

_____

_____

_____

_____

_____

_____

_____

_____

_____

* Remember to check your spelling, grammar, and punctuation.

This page will not be scored.

SSG114   ISBN: 9781487704032 © On The Mark Press

Writing an Article

Write your article here.

_____
(Headline)

_____   _____
_____   _____
_____   _____
_____   _____
_____   _____
_____   _____
_____   _____
_____   _____
_____   _____
_____   _____
_____   _____
_____   _____
_____   _____
_____   _____
_____   _____
_____   _____
_____   _____

SSG114   ISBN: 9781487704032 © On The Mark Press

Writing Multiple Choice

12. Choose the best opening sentence for the following paragraph.

_____.
They created a mixture of bee's wax, Arabic gum, egg whites, and gelatin. Then they added crushed petals from roses, orchids, and other flowers. The polish was applied to the nails and left to dry overnight.

- ○ In ancient times, nail colour was used to show social status.
- ○ The Chinese are given credit for inventing the first real "nail polish."
- ○ Members of the Chinese royal family liked to use gold and silver on their nails.
- ○ A henna stain was also used to colour nails.

13. Choose the punctuation that is missing from the following sentence.

The spring flowers are starting to bloom, said my neighbour.

- ○ question mark
- ○ apostrophe
- ○ exclamation mark
- ○ quotation marks

14. Choose the word in the following sentence that is described by the word "hungry."

The volunteers at the shelter saw that the kitties were hungry, the puppies needed exercise and the two birds were unhappy.

- ○ puppies
- ○ kitties
- ○ volunteers
- ○ birds

15. Choose the sentence that is written correctly.

- ○ "Haven't you finished the test, Troy?" the teacher asked.
- ○ "Haven't you finished the test Troy?" the teacher asked.
- ○ "Haven't you finished the test, Troy," the teacher asked?
- ○ "Havent you finished the test, Troy?" the teacher asked.

Freshwater Habitats

Only 3% of the water on Earth is freshwater. Most of that is frozen solid in ice and glaciers. Some of its underground. About 1% of the remaining freshwater makes up the worlds rivers, streams, lakes, ponds, and wetlands. Each of these places is home to specific types of animals and vegetation that thrive in that particular environment.

LAKES & PONDS

Location: Lakes and ponds are bodies of water that come in many different sizes and can be found on all the continents on Earth.

Vegetation: Algae, Cattails, Reeds & Rushes, Plankton, Pond Weeds, Willow Trees

Animals: Freshwater Fish, Ducks & Geese, Turtles & Frogs, Dragonflies

RIVERS & STREAMS

Location: Rivers and streams are flowing bodies of water that move in one direction. They come in many shapes and sizes and can be found on continents all over the world.

Vegetation: Algae, Cattails, Reeds & Rushes, Plankton

Animals: Freshwater Fish, Frogs & Salamanders, Egrets & Herons, Otters

WETLANDS

Location: Wetlands are areas of standing water thick with vegetation. They are part land and part water. Marshes, swamps, and bogs are all wetlands. Wetlands are found on continents all over the world.

Vegetation: Reeds & Sedges, Marsh Grasses, Pond Lilies, Cyprus & Gum Trees, Mangrove Trees

Animals: Snakes, Turtles & Frogs, Herons, Fish & Shellfish, Muskrats, Dragonflies & Mosquitoes

SSG114   ISBN: 9781487704032 © On The Mark Press

Freshwater Habitats: Questions

1. What does the term "1%" refer to in the opening paragraph?

   ○ the amount of freshwater on Earth

   ○ the amount of freshwater that is frozen solid in ice and glaciers

   ○ the amount of freshwater in the world's rivers, streams, lakes, ponds, and wetlands

   ○ the amount of freshwater that is underground

2. Which type of habitat is described in the following description?

   "flowing bodies of water in many shapes and sizes that move in one direction"

   ○ lakes & ponds

   ○ glaciers

   ○ wetlands

   ○ rivers & streams

3. What type of vegetation is common to all three habitats?

   ○ algae

   ○ reeds

   ○ plankton

   ○ cattails

4. What type of habitat is part land and part water?

   ○ wetlands

   ○ lakes

   ○ rivers

   ○ ponds

5. What animal is common to all three habitats?

   ○ turtles

   ○ dragonflies

   ○ frogs

   ○ ducks

Freshwater Habitats: Questions

6. Why do you think dragonflies and mosquitoes are attracted to wetlands? Use specific information from the text and your own ideas to support your answer.

_____

_____

_____

_____

_____

_____

_____

_____

_____

_____

7. Which of these habitats would you most like to visit? Explain your answer.

_____

_____

_____

_____

_____

_____

_____

_____

_____

_____

_____

_____

SSG114   ISBN: 9781487704032 © On The Mark Press

Writing a Movie Review

8. Choose a movie that you have seen recently or in the past – either on TV or in a theatre – and write a review of that movie. Include the name of the movie, what the movie is about, who was in the movie, and why you liked or disliked the movie.

Ideas for my Movie Review

_____

_____

_____

_____

_____

_____

_____

_____

_____

_____

* Remember to check your spelling, grammar and punctuation.

This page will not be scored.

SSG114   ISBN: 9781487704032 © On The Mark Press

Writing a Movie Review

Write your movie review here.

SSG114 ISBN: 9781487704032 © On The Mark Press

Writing Multiple Choice

9. Choose the best order for the following sentences to create a paragraph.

   (1) Four square miles of downtown Johnstown were completely destroyed.

   (2) On May 31, 1889, a dam broke above Johnstown, Pennsylvania.

   (3) Houses, trees, animals, and over 2000 people were swept away.

   (4) About 3:00 p.m., a huge wall of water more than seven metres high raced down the valley.

   ◯ 1, 3, 4, 2

   ◯ 2, 4, 3, 1

   ◯ 3, 1, 2, 4

   ◯ 2, 3, 1, 4

10. Which part of speech identifies the underlined words in the following sentence?

    The noon train <u>was thundering</u> around the bend.

    ◯ noun phrase

    ◯ adjective phrase

    ◯ verb phrase

    ◯ adverb phrase

11. Which sentence does not belong in the following paragraph?

    (1) My family arrived to volunteer at the food bank at 2:00 in the afternoon. (2) Many organizations or schools run food drives. (3) A woman named Ann led us into a gigantic open room. (4) In the centre of the room were dozens of stainless steel tables lined up like desks in a classroom.

    ◯ Sentence 1

    ◯ Sentence 2

    ◯ Sentence 3

    ◯ Sentence 4

12. Choose the correct words to complete the following sentence.

    _____ I go home, I _____ need to stop at the store.

    ◯ Before, still

    ◯ After, should

    ◯ When, almost

    ◯ Because, might

Writing Multiple Choice

13. Which sentence best completes the following paragraph?

    What's the best way to keep children healthy in school? Frequent hand-washing is the simplest and most effective way to stay healthy. Children should wash their hands before eating and after going to the bathroom, blowing their noses or playing outside.

    _____

    ○ Kids should soap up for as long as it takes to sing "Happy Birthday" twice.

    ○ Many childhood illnesses are caused by viruses.

    ○ Remind children not to share water bottles.

    ○ In the early school years, a child's immune system is put to the test.

14. Which word or words are best suited to complete the following sentence?

    We _____ at the beach yesterday.

    ○ are

    ○ used to be

    ○ were

    ○ had gone

15. Choose the word that has the same meaning as the underlined word in the following sentence.

    As the owl flapped its wings quickly, it found itself <u>buoyed</u> upwards.

    ○ flying

    ○ spinning

    ○ speeding

    ○ lifted

16. Choose the sentence that is written correctly.

    ○ Marsha's daughter will set the table; we'll cook dinner.

    ○ Marshas' daughter will set the table; we'll cook dinner.

    ○ Marsha's daughter will set the table: we'll cook dinner.

    ○ Marsha's daughter will set the table, we'll cook dinner!

SSG114   ISBN: 9781487704032 © On The Mark Press

The Dog and the Shadow

By Richard S. Sharpe

A hungry dog some meat seized,
And, with the ample booty pleased,
His neighbour dogs forsook;
In fear for his delightful prize,
He look'd around with eager eyes,   5
And ran to cross the brook.

To cross the brook, a single plank
Was simply laid from bank to bank;
And, as he passed alone,
He saw his shadow at his feet,   10
Which seem'd another dog, with meat
Much better than his own.

Ah, ha! Thought he, as no one spies,
If I could make this piece my prize,
I should be a double winner;   15
So made a snatch; when sad to tell!
His own piece in the water fell,
And thus he lost his dinner.

The fable which above you see,
To greedy folks must useful be,   20
And suits those to a tittle,
Who long for what they can't obtain;
'Tis sure far wiser to remain
Contented with a little.

LINE

The Dog and the Shadow: Questions

1. Line 1 rhymes with Line 2. Which line does line 3 rhyme with?

   ○ Line 5

   ○ Line 6

   ○ Line 4

   ○ Line 2

2. What confused the dog as he was crossing the brook?

   ○ another dog

   ○ his dinner

   ○ his shadow

   ○ his neighbour

3. The word "snatch" as used in line 16 means

   ○ to grab quickly.

   ○ to move secretly.

   ○ to take a small amount.

   ○ to lose something.

4. Why did the dog lose his dinner?

   ○ He was lazy.

   ○ He was clumsy.

   ○ He was greedy.

   ○ He was silly.

5. Which of the following words is most suited to be used instead of "fable" in line 19?

   ○ myth

   ○ report

   ○ story

   ○ poem

6. Which line rhymes with line 24?

   ○ line 20

   ○ line 21

   ○ line 22

   ○ line 23

SSG114   ISBN: 9781487704032 © On The Mark Press

The Dog and the Shadow: Questions

7. How can you tell that this is not a modern poem? Use specific details from the text and your own ideas to support your answer.

_____

_____

_____

_____

_____

_____

_____

_____

_____

8. What is the moral taught in this poem? Use information from the text and your own ideas to support your answer.

_____

_____

_____

_____

_____

_____

_____

_____

_____

Writing a Description

9. Describe your favourite holiday meal. Include what holiday you are writing about, what kinds of food, how the food smells and tastes and how it is cooked and served.

Ideas for my Description

_____

_____

_____

_____

_____

_____

_____

_____

_____

_____

_____

_____

_____

* Remember to check your spelling, grammar, and punctuation.

This page will not be scored.

SSG114   ISBN: 9781487704032 © On The Mark Press

Writing a Description

Write your description here.

_____

_____

_____

_____

_____

_____

_____

_____

_____

_____

_____

_____

_____

_____

_____

_____

_____

Do not write in this area.

SSG114   ISBN: 9781487704032 © On The Mark Press

Writing Multiple Choice

10. Choose the best opening sentence for this paragraph.

    _____. Each pride of lions has its own area. Their area is usually in open, sandy country with a few trees for shade. The male lions protect this rea. A full-grown male can weigh 204 kilograms and be 3 metres long.

    ○ Lions hunt antelopes, zebras, pigs and sometimes giraffe.

    ○ After eating, a lion will take a long nap.

    ○ Lions like to live in groups called prides.

    ○ Lions like to be left alone.

11. Which phrase has the same meaning as the underlined word in the following sentence?

    The astronaut had to <u>navigate</u> the space shuttle.

    ○ lower the wheels

    ○ plan the direction

    ○ measure the width

    ○ measure the speed

12. Choose the phrase that best completes the following analogy.

    <u>Sun</u> is to <u>star</u> as

    ○ stars are to planets

    ○ comet is to tail

    ○ moon is to Earth

    ○ Mars is to planet

13. Choose the word that is a suitable synonym for the underlined word in the following sentence.

    Johnathan is <u>apt</u> to return from school shortly.

    ○ likely

    ○ unlikely

    ○ willing

    ○ unwilling

SSG114   ISBN: 9781487704032 © On The Mark Press

Writing: Correct the Sentences

14. Edit and make corrections to the following sentences.

a. I don't want no ice cream.

_____

b. Teddy can't go nowhere for now.

_____

c. It really doesnt' go no farther.

_____

d. I just love german chocolate cake said Maria.

_____

e. Dr J Walley is now here.

_____

f. Marla don't want homework.

_____

g. I didnt do nothing wrong.

_____

The Castle that Love Built

Imagine creating a dream house for the love of your life! That is exactly what George Boldt did for his beloved wife, Louise.

George Boldt was born into a poor family in 1851 in Prussia. When he was 13 years old, he left Germany for the New World. First, he worked in restaurants and hotels in New York City. Next, he tried farming in Texas but was unsuccessful. He returned to New York in 1871, then moved to Philadelphia. There he met Louise Kehrer and it was love at first sight! Although Louise was only 15 years old, she and George were married. They had two children, George Jr. and Louise (Clover).

2

George began his hotel career in a low level position, but his intelligence and hard work paved the way to greater success. He became manager and part owner of the world famous Waldorf-Astoria Hotel in New York City. Later, he purchased the Bellevue-Stratford in Philadelphia. As his personal fortune grew, he had the financial means to realize some of his lifetime dreams.

At the time, the Thousand Islands were a popular summer vacation spot for the wealthy people of New York and Philadelphia. In 1865, the Boldts purchased Hart Island, one of the many islands found in the St. Lawrence River which separates Ontario, Canada and New York State.

The Boldts made a number of changes to their island. They actually reshaped the island into a heart shape and renamed it "Heart Island." A popular story is that this new shape was to celebrate George's love for Louise. Their summer home on the island was one of the largest and grandest in the area.

5

But George wanted more than just having the largest and grandest home. He decided to build a fairy tale castle. In the winter of 1899, their "cottage" was hauled across the ice to nearby Wellesley Island. In 1900, George set plans in motion to start his ambitious project. The castle, designed after the 16th century landmark castles in Europe, was to rise six stories from the ground level of the indoor swimming pool to the highest tower room. There would be 127 rooms, including 30 bathrooms.

SSG114   ISBN: 9781487704032 © On The Mark Press

An elevator would assist the inhabitants of the mansion. An underground passageway led from a dock at the water's edge. This would allow the servants to bring the goods, transported to the island by barge, to the storage rooms in the castle. 7

A formal Italian garden was designed to feature a fountain pool, a terrace and marble statues. Many of the materials were imported from Europe as George spared no expense on his dream house for Louise. He invested $2.5 million, a huge fortune for the times, to launch such a project. 8

As a certain token of his love for Louise, he planned to present her with the fairy tale home on Valentine's Day. But fate intervened... and tragedy struck! 9

In January 1904, Louise suffered a heart attack and suddenly died. She was only 41 years old. Even though Louise was known to be in "delicate health," George was totally unprepared for such a devastating blow! Understandably, he was heartbroken. The reason for his dream ended with her death. He telegrammed his construction crew (300 craftsmen and workers) and ordered all work to cease immediately. 10

George never returned to the island. The unfinished castle was a reminder to a love story that had a tragic ending. For 73 years, the castle and the other existing stone structures were at the mercy of the elements, both nature and man. Wind, ice, and snow took their toll. Vandals damaged the interior and exterior of the main house and outbuildings. 11

Luckily, this deterioration came to an end in 1977. Heart Island and the nearby Boldt Yacht House were purchased by the Thousand Island Bridge Authority for $1.00 U.S. The agreement stated that all money earned from opening the castle to the public would be used for restoration. In the years since then, more than $15 million have been spent to restore and upgrade the castle. Work continues each year, following George's original plans as closely as possible. 12

Boldt Castle has become a popular attraction in the Thousand Islands. The first level has been turned into a museum, with exhibits dedicated to the lives of George and Louise Boldt. Visitors can reach the castle by water taxi, tour boats, and private boats. The five-acre island hosts several other buildings that were built to serve the castle that was built as a labor of love over a century ago. 13

The Castle that Love Built: Questions

1. Why is paragraph 2 important to the story?

   ○ It tells about hotels in New York City.

   ○ It tells about George's early years.

   ○ It tells about George's dream.

   ○ It gives a description of Louise.

2. What happened when George first met Louise?

   ○ They didn't like each other at first.

   ○ He took her on a date.

   ○ It was love at first sight!

   ○ They moved to New York.

3. What does paragraph 3 tell the readers about George?

   ○ He was not very successful at first.

   ○ He was intelligent and hard working.

   ○ He had two children.

   ○ He loved Louise.

4. Where was Hart Island located? (paragraph 4)

   ○ Philadelphia

   ○ New York City

   ○ Hudson River

   ○ St. Lawrence River

5. What is described in paragraph 6?

   ○ the fairy tale castle

   ○ the large, grand summer home

   ○ Wellesley Island

   ○ Heart Island

SSG114   ISBN: 9781487704032 © On The Mark Press

The Castle that Love Built: Questions

6. How were the servants going to get from the dock at the water's edge to the storage rooms in the castle?

   ○ They were going to use an elevator.

   ○ They were going to use an underground passageway.

   ○ They were going to walk along a path from the dock.

   ○ They were going to take a boat.

7. Which of the following would be an appropriate subheading for paragraph 10?

   ○ A Fairy Tale Castle

   ○ The House on Heart Island

   ○ The Death of a Dream

   ○ Building a Castle

8. What was supposed to happen on Valentine's Day?

   ○ George was going to give Louise a large bunch of flowers.

   ○ George was going to present Louise with the fairy tale castle.

   ○ George was going to take Louise on a trip.

   ○ George was going to invest $2.5 million dollars in the castle.

9. What does the word "deterioration" mean as used in paragraph 12?

   ○ the process of becoming progressively worse

   ○ the process of becoming progressively better

   ○ to turn away from

   ○ to abandon something

10. How much did the Thousand Island Bridge Authority pay for Heart Island and the Boldt Yacht House?

    ○ $15 million dollars

    ○ $100

    ○ $2.5 million dollars

    ○ $1.00

The Castle that Love Built: Questions

11. Why do you think George Boldt never returned to Heart Island? Use specific details from the text and your own ideas to support your answer.

_____

_____

_____

_____

_____

_____

_____

_____

_____

12. What happened to Boldt Castle after the Thousand Island Bridge Authority purchased it? Use specific details from the text to support your answer.

_____

_____

_____

_____

_____

_____

_____

_____

_____

SSG114   ISBN: 9781487704032 © On The Mark Press

Writing Instructions

13. Think of a game you like to play – a card game, board game or video game, etc. – and write instructions on how to play that game.

> Ideas for my Instructions

_____

_____

_____

_____

_____

_____

_____

_____

_____

_____

_____

_____

_____

* Remember to check your spelling, grammar, and punctuation.

This page will not be scored.

Writing Instructions

Write your instructions here.

SSG114   ISBN: 9781487704032 © On The Mark Press

Writing Multiple Choice

14. Which of the following sentences is written correctly?

    ○ Yes Terry, there are thirty-one days in July.

    ○ Yes, Terry, there are thirty one days in July.

    ○ Yes, Terry, there are thirty-one days in July.

    ○ Yes Terry there are thirty one days in July.

15. Choose the best opening sentence for the following paragraph.

    _____. They run along the west coast of South America. They are about 8000 kilometres long. The go through seven countries.

    ○ The Andes are the world's longest chain of mountains.

    ○ Most people in the Andes farm and raise animals.

    ○ The Andes has many types of plants and animals.

    ○ The rugged land of the Andes makes travelling hard.

16. Choose the word or words that complete the following sentence correctly.

    Antonio is _____ than Jaheim.

    ○ most careful

    ○ careful

    ○ very careful

    ○ more careful

17. Choose the correct order to make a paragraph using the sentences below.

    (1) The dog started to bark.
    (2) When lightning filled the sky before the second boom, I was relieved it was just a storm!
    (3) A loud boom woke me up!
    (4) I was worried it was some kind of explosion.

    ○ 4, 3, 1, 2

    ○ 3, 1, 4, 2

    ○ 1, 2, 3, 4

    ○ 2, 1, 4, 3

THE CITY NEWS

Local Girl Earns Medal for Volunteering

BY HILARY BINNS

Michaela Parkington, a sixth grade 1 student at George Washington Middle School, was awarded a youth medal for three years of volunteer service at the local Guide Dog Training Centre. The ceremony of honour took place at the Morgantown City Hall on Friday afternoon. For the past three years, Michaela has been part of the training centre's puppy raising program.

Guide dogs are chosen carefully from 2 birth. Most of the dogs are Labrador Retrievers, German Sheperds, or Golden Retrievers. At eight weeks of age, the puppies are placed in homes that will care for them until they are old enough to begin the intense guide dog training program.

Michaela and her family have now 3 helped raise two future guide dogs. They have their third puppy in their home now. "It's the very best volunteer job in the world," Michaela said. "The puppies are adorable. I get to keep them for about a year and a half. My job is to give the puppy lots of personal contact. I have to get the puppy used to everyday situations. That means lots of walks and car rides but mostly it means lots of playing. I also help teach them basic commands like 'sit', 'stay', or 'lie down', but I don't give them any official guide dog training. That's what they do at the centre."

Exposing puppies to a variety of 4 things is the key to raising a successful guide dog. For example, puppy raisers are asked to feed the puppies from different shaped containers (square, circular, rectangular) as well as containers

SSG114 ISBN: 9781487704032 © On The Mark Press

THE CITY NEWS

made of different materials (metal, plastic, paper, clay, etc.). Even offering the puppy a wobbly water dish one day and a heavy dish the next day is a great learning experience.

Puppy raisers must walk the puppies on different surfaces such as bark, grass, tall weeds, pavement, tile, mud and carpet. 5

Future guide dogs also need to be exposed to other dogs and animals as well as other people. Even exposure to things like fast moving objects is important in raising a guide dog. The puppies need to see things like skateboard riders, scooters, children running and playing soccer, and even vacuum cleaners and shopping carts. 6

"Every time we give the puppy a new experience we watch him or her very carefully," Michaela said. "We don't want the puppy to be scared. If he looks scared, we stop the activity right away if possible. Then we pick up the puppy and make sure he is okay." 7

Twice a month, Michaela and her dad bring the puppy into the Guide Dog Training Centre where the puppy works with specialists who monitor the puppy's progress. 8

Paul Stone, a trainer at the Morgantown Guide Dog Centre, said that Michaela is one of their best volunteers. "She is a perfect puppy trainer," he said. "Michaela does everything we ask her to do. She takes her volunteer role very seriously. All of us appreciate that." 9

Michaela admitted that her role as a puppy raiser is hard at times. "Some days it feels like a big responsibility. Many times, I really want to hang out with my friends after school, but I can't because I have to go home and take the puppy outside. The puppy isn't allowed outdoors by himself. He has to be on a leash and watched carefully." 10

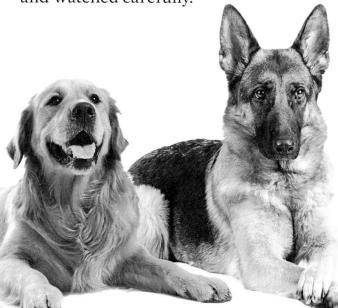

SSG114   ISBN: 9781487704032 © On The Mark Press

THE CITY NEWS

Michaela said that the worst part of **11** this volunteer role is returning the dog to the training centre after the puppy raising period has ended. "I have cried every time," she said. "The puppies become part of my family, so it's really hard to day good-bye."

When the puppies are returned to **12** the Guide Dog Training Centre, they are tested once again. Those dogs that pass the tests begin formal training with guide dog instructors. After four to six months of rigorous training, the dogs have learned how to assist their future blind, deaf, or disabled owner.

Paul Stone said, "Every **13** puppy Michaela has worked with has become a fantastic guide dog. That says so much about her commitment to these animals and to our program."

"Even though it's really **14** hard to give the puppies back," Michaela said, "I know that what I'm doing is important. I like the fact that I am helping raise a guide dog. I always try to think of the person who will receive such a great dog. I know that in a small way, I have helped a blind or deaf person gain more independence. That helps with my sadness."

Does Michaela see herself becom- **15** ing a certified Guide Dog Trainer when she grows up? "I definitely want to work with animals," she answered. "I'm thinking of becoming a veterinarian, but a guide dog trainer would be fun, too."

 SSG114   ISBN: 9781487704032 © On The Mark Press

Local Girl Earns Medal for Volunteering: Questions

1. According to paragraph 1, why was Michaela getting a medal?

   ○ She had volunteered for two years at the local food bank.

   ○ She had volunteered for two years at the local animal shelter.

   ○ She had volunteered for three years at the Guide Dog Training Centre.

   ○ She had volunteered for three years at the animal hospital.

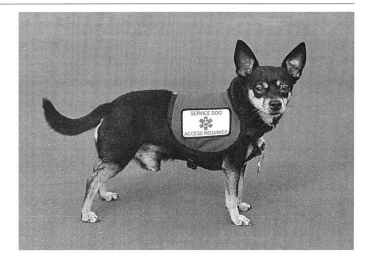

2. What is the main purpose of paragraph 3?

   ○ to explain what Michaela's job is as a volunteer

   ○ to tell about the puppies in the training program

   ○ to tell about the Guide Dog Training Centre

   ○ to explain why it's important to volunteer

3. What does the word "wobbly" mean as used in paragraph 4?

   ○ to tip over

   ○ to sway gently in the breeze

   ○ to stay firmly on the ground

   ○ to move from side to side in an unsteady way

4. What happens if the puppy gets scared during a training session?

   ○ They continue on with the training.

   ○ They stop the activity and pick up the puppy.

   ○ They train the puppy to not be afraid.

   ○ They have the puppy do the activity again.

Local Girl Earns Medal for Volunteering: Questions

5. What does Paul Stone think of Michaela as a volunteer?

   ○ He thinks she should work harder.

   ○ He thinks she should train other volunteers.

   ○ He thinks she is a perfect puppy trainer.

   ○ He thinks she is too young to train puppies.

6. How often do Michaela and her dad bring the puppy to the Guide Dog Training Centre?

   ○ once a week

   ○ twice a month

   ○ once a month

   ○ twice a week

7. What is the worst part of volunteering for Michaela?

   ○ returning the puppy to the centre when the puppy raising period is over

   ○ walking the puppy every day

   ○ missing out on playing sports

   ○ not getting to hang out with her friends

8. What does the word "certified" mean as used in paragraph 15?

   ○ to officially be recognized as having specific qualifications

   ○ to officially be declared unable to care for yourself

   ○ to officially be declared a volunteer

   ○ to fail to complete or meet certain standards

9. What happens after the puppies are returned to the Guide Dog Training Centre?

   ○ They learn how to walk without a leash.

   ○ They begin formal training with guide dog instructors.

   ○ They miss the family that has been raising them.

   ○ They learn how to play with other puppies.

SSG114   ISBN: 9781487704032 © On The Mark Press

Local Girl Earns Medal for Volunteering: Questions

10. Why do you think it's important for puppies, that are being raised to be guide dogs, to be exposed to a wide variety of situations? Use specific details from the story and your own ideas to support your answer.

_____

_____

_____

_____

_____

_____

_____

_____

_____

11. Do you think Michaela might be a good veterinarian when she grows up? Explain why or why not. Use details from the story and your own ideas to support your answer.

_____

_____

_____

_____

_____

_____

_____

_____

_____

_____

Writing: Correct Punctuation

12. Rewrite the following paragraphs adding the correct punctuation.

What a gorgeous day exclaimed Melissa Do you want to go for a hike in the canyon we can pack a lunch and take the dogs

Sure answered Keira I ll bring sandwiches cookies trail mix and water if you can bring treats for the dogs its 9 00 a m now when would you like to leave

Lets see if we can be ready in an hour said Melissa

Write your corrected paragraphs here.

_____

_____

_____

_____

_____

_____

_____

_____

_____

_____

_____

_____

_____

_____

SSG114   ISBN: 9781487704032 © On The Mark Press

Writing Multiple Choice

13. Choose the sentence that does not belong in the following paragraph.

    (1) It's the first day of summer vacation and the sun is shining. (2) I feel very happy and free, like anything is possible! (3) My little brother is being a brat. (4) My friend Richie is coming over and our summer adventures are about to begin!

    ○ Sentence 1

    ○ Sentence 2

    ○ Sentence 3

    ○ Sentence 4

14. Choose the correct word to complete the following sentence.

    _____ you planning a trip to Paris?

    ○ Will

    ○ Are

    ○ So

    ○ Is

15. Choose the words that best describe the underlined word.

    There is a <u>curvature</u> to the wings.

    ○ a circular form

    ○ a sharp angle

    ○ a back drop

    ○ a smooth arc

16. Which is the best way to combine the information in the following sentences?

    You will need an umbrella.

    Spring weather is unpredictable.

    It can start out sunny and suddenly start to rain.

    ○ Take an umbrella since unpredictable spring weather can start out sunny and suddenly turn to rain.

    ○ Spring weather can start out sunny, and suddenly start to rain, you will need an umbrella

    ○ Take an umbrella in the spring, it can start out sunny, it can turn rainy.

    ○ Spring weather is unpredictable, take an umbrella.

Writing Multiple Choice

17. Choose the punctuation that is missing from the following sentence.

    Lets take the boat and go to the Horseshoe Lake today.

    - ○ quotation marks
    - ○ exclamation mark
    - ○ comma
    - ○ apostrophe

18. Choose the word in the following sentence that is described by the word "expensive".

    The meal that Alex and Jenny want to order at the restaurant will be very expensive.

    - ○ Alex
    - ○ restaurant
    - ○ meal
    - ○ Jenny

19. Choose the part of speech that identifies the underlined word in the following sentence.

    Mr. and Mrs. Martinez travelled to London <u>recently</u>.

    - ○ adjective
    - ○ adverb
    - ○ noun
    - ○ verb

20. Choose the best the best opening sentence for the following paragraph.

    _____. The twin brothers grew up in Maple Ridge, Canada, a suburb of Vancouver. They became interested in real estate at an early age. They have turned that interest and their considerable talent into four popular home renovation shows on HGTV.

    - ○ They learned firsthand how to go after big goals.
    - ○ Jonathan and Drew Scott are two ambitious Canadians who have made it big in the U.S.
    - ○ Growing up, the brothers always knew they were different.
    - ○ Drew and Jonathan bought their first home when they were just 18.

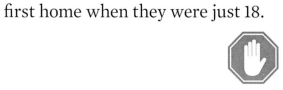

 SSG114   ISBN: 9781487704032 © On The Mark Press

Grandma's Secret

"Come Jen," my mother called me. "I need your help today.
We need to clean Grandma's house and pack some things away."
I thought of Grandma Ella, no longer living on her own
Her mind and body weary, she's in a nursing home.

We drive up to the old house, weathered and so worn   5
Reminds me of Grandma Ella, a thought I find forlorn.
I look out in the backyard where all we kids would play
The sand pile and the swing set, it seems like yesterday.

I loved those summer visits. Oh, the stories Gram would share.
She cooked and cared for all of us, it seemed, without a care.   10
She'd say "It makes me happy to share all of your love."
"I know that Grandpa's watching us high up from above."

My Grandpa, just like Grandma, was what they call "old school"
Always helping others and living the Golden Rule
Suddenly Grandpa left us, without a real goodbye   15
But Grandma, in her wisdom, encouraged us to cry.

I help mom in the kitchen. We sort through things and pack
Neither of us saying we know Gram won't be back.
"I'm going to the attic," I call out as I leave
But what I'm really looking for is a quiet place to grieve.   20

I climb the stairs while thinking "I wonder what I'll find"
Some treasure or a memory that time has left behind.
Over in the corner, half hidden from my view
A battered looking hat box my attention drew.

It was scratched and it was dusty, but still I want to look   25
I tugged the lid so gently, like opening a book.
Piles and piles of letters, tied up with ribbon blue,
Old names, old stamps, old writing, were the only clue.

LINE

Some letters were for Grandma from places long ago.
Some letters, in her writing, were for a name I did not know.   30
It seemed like an invasion just to start to read
But somehow deep inside me, it was an aching need.

The letters told the story of a young love, oh, so strong
In spite of all life's troubles, nothing could go wrong.
But then, the Great War started, and Grandma's beau was far away   35
For he would serve his country and he'd return some day.

Those letters were Gram's lifeline to a world so far away,
Where young men fought so fiercely and with their lives did pay.
Each day, Gram had no real choice except to wait and wait
And hope that death would not become her soldier's final fate.   40

But there, a government letter, at the bottom of the pile
I waited to unfold it, knowing the contents all the while.
It began, "We regret to inform you . . ." I felt a sudden tear
For it held news for Grandma, oh so hard to hear.

I sat there just reflecting on all that I had read.   45
At once, a hundred questions were whirling in my head.
I tried to make some sense of this and then it was so clear.
My Grandma's love, her soldier boy, was such a memory dear.

Gram loved my Grandpa dearly, she was proud to be his wife,
Looking after him and family was the focus of her life.   50
No one had ever mentioned this soldier from the past,
A secret that was hidden but now was told at last.

I heard my mother calling as she looked for me.
I gathered up the letters, afraid that she would see.
Soon she walked toward me and then I saw her smile.   55
"I see you found Gram's letters. They've been there a while."

She must have seen my shocked look and surprise upon my face
And then she helped me to restore Gram's letters to their place.
"Some day when you are older, I'm sure you'll understand
That past events and present, sometimes go hand in hand."   60

SSG114 ISBN: 9781487704032 © On The Mark Press

"The soldier boy that Gram once loved more than any other
Was like another kind, good man . . . for he was Grandpa's brother.
Gramps made a vow that he would care for Grandma from the start
And soon his love and all that care, won your Grandma's heart."

"I think she kept the letters, though many years have past,   65
  As some kind of reminder that her new love would last.
  One day when you are older, and your true love you find,
  I'm sure that Grandma's story will come into your mind."

I thought of Grandma's secret, one that my mother knew
  And wondered if my mother had her past secrets, too.   70

Grandma's Secret: Questions

1. What word is used in the poem to rhyme with "worn" in line 5?

   ○ sworn

   ○ torn

   ○ forlorn

   ○ born

2. Where had Jen's Grandma Ella gone?

   ○ to a nursing home

   ○ to the hospital

   ○ to her vacation house

   ○ to her daughter's house

3. Why does Jen go to the attic? (line 19)

   ○ to sort through things and pack

   ○ to help her mother

   ○ to find her grandma

   ○ to find a quiet place to grieve

4. What does the word "battered" mean as used in line 24?

   ○ stirred up

   ○ not in good shape

   ○ something that has been hit over and over again

   ○ someone who had just batted

5. How did Jen feel about reading her Grandma's letters?

   ○ She felt guilty.

   ○ She felt happy.

   ○ She felt an aching need.

   ○ She felt silly.

6. What does the word "beau" refer to in line 35?

   ○ Grandma's first love

   ○ Grandpa when he was young

   ○ Grandma's brother

   ○ Grandma's neighbour who was a soldier

SSG114   ISBN: 9781487704032 © On The Mark Press

Grandma's Secret: Questions

7. What does the word "lifeline" describe in line line 37?

   ○ the world so far away

   ○ Gram's letters

   ○ Gram's soldier boy

   ○ the Great War

8. How did Jen look when she found out her mom knew about Gram's letters?

   ○ angry and upset

   ○ happy

   ○ confused

   ○ shocked and surprised

9. When does Jen's mom think Jen will understand about Gram's secret?

   ○ tomorrow

   ○ next week

   ○ when she is older

   ○ in a year or so

10. What happened to Gram's soldier boy?

    ○ he moved away

    ○ he died in the Great War

    ○ he broke up with her

    ○ he got hurt in the Great War

11. Who was Gram's soldier boy to Grandpa?

    ○ his cousin

    ○ his uncle

    ○ his brother

    ○ his friend

12. What word is used in the poem to rhyme with "heart" in line 64?

    ○ smart

    ○ start

    ○ dart

    ○ tart

Grandma's Secret: Questions

13. Retell this story in ten lines or less. Be sure to include all the important facts. Use details from the poem to support your answer.

_____

_____

_____

_____

_____

_____

_____

_____

_____

_____

14 Reread the last two lines of this poem. What do you think the author is trying to say about the people in our lives? Use details from the poem and your own ideas to support your answer.

_____

_____

_____

_____

_____

_____

_____

_____

_____

_____

SSG114   ISBN: 9781487704032 © On The Mark Press

Writing a Poem

15. Write a poem about your favourite season of the year. Use the same rhyming pattern as in *Grandma's Secret*.

Ideas for my Poem

_____

_____

_____

_____

_____

_____

_____

_____

_____

_____

_____

_____

_____

* Remember to check your grammar, spelling, and punctuation. And make sure your rhyming words make sense.

This page will not be scored.

Writing a Poem

Write your poem here.

_____

_____

_____

_____

_____

_____

_____

_____

_____

_____

_____

_____

_____

_____

_____

_____

_____

_____

_____

_____

_____

SSG114   ISBN: 9781487704032 © On The Mark Press

The History of Some Popular Foods

A number of food inventions were unplanned and unintentional. Many of today's favourite foods were discovered by accident. While most inventors are smart, the truly alert ones can recognize that what appears to be a mistake can be turned into a new idea. Take a peek at some basic foods that might be in your lunch today. You may have some that were invented accidentally.

1

The Sandwich

During the Middle Ages, thick slices of coarse bread were used in place of plates. Meat and other food were heaped upon the bread and eaten with the fingers. The thick bread absorbed the juices and, at the end of the meal, one might eat the soggy bread. If one was full, the bread was tossed to the dogs or thrown out back of the kitchen where the poor would retrieve and eat it.

2

The first written record of the word 'sandwich" appeared in 1762. The story says that John Montagu, the Fourth Earl of Sandwich, was busy gambling with some friends in his English gaming house. He had been at the table for twenty-four hours and didn't want to take time out to eat. When the servants brought the food, he ordered them to place all of the meat between slices of bread. In this way, he could eat and still have one hand free to carry on with his bets. That's how he (or his servants) invented the sandwich! Even though people had probably eaten a form of sandwiches before, once they were given a famous name, they became very popular. Today, they are eaten everywhere in the world in some form or other.

3

The true origins of yogurt is uncertain as even the most ancient records mention it. The practice of keeping liquids in goatskins or other containers made of an animal's skin or stomach lends itself to this simple food production. When the milk is left in contact with air some of the bacteria would cause the milk to coagulate and ferment. One legend tells of a shepherd who forgot milk for some time in his goatskin and when he remembered it, found a creamy tasty treat!

4

Another story says that a Turkish nomad, travelling in a mountain region, was carrying a goatskin containing milk. At the end of his voyage, he discovered that the temperature and bacteria in the

5

Yogurt

goatskin had transformed the milk into a creamy beverage. Yogurut or joggurt means "thick milk" in the Turkish language. We have probably taken our modern term yogurt from this word. The benefits of eating yogurt are many and it is popular the world over. It is produced with many flavours and added ingredients such as fruit.

According to history, pretzels were first invented by monks in seventh-century France. They rolled sourdough into string-like pieces and then folded them into the crossover shape. Then the peculiar shapes were baked. It was one monk's idea that these shapes represented arms folded in prayer, so he thought that these snacks could be used as a reward to give children for learning their prayers. The word "pretzel" comes from the Latin word pretiola which means "little reward." A good pretzel can still be considered a reward today!

6

Potato chips are likely one of the most popular snacks today. They are made in a variety of shapes and flavours. Many other salty snack foods are fashioned after this invention. In 1853, a chef named George Crum worked in a resort in Saratoga Springs, New York. Many wealthy people vacationed there.

7

One customer kept sending back his plate of friend potatoes, asking that they be sliced thinner and deep-fried longer. George was a man with a temper who felt he was too busy for such a whim so he decided to teach the complainer a lesson. He sliced the potatoes very thin, fried them crispy and salted them. To George's surprise, the diner was so delighted that he asked for more. These potatoes were known as Saratoga Chips until the early 1900's when other versions of the snack began to appear.

8

We have such a variety of food and snacks available to us that we take them for granted. Those that are extensions of early foods were probably designed to be new. But the original foods were most likely invented by accident and became popular because of their taste and appeal.

9

SSG114   ISBN: 9781487704032 © On The Mark Press

The History of Some Popular Foods: Questions

1. Which popular food was invented while people were gambling?

   ○ Yogurt

   ○ Sandwiches

   ○ Pretzels

   ○ Potato Chips

2. What do the words "coagulate and ferment" mean as they are used in paragraph 4?

   ○ to come together in an excited way

   ○ to make milk a runny substance that needs to be thickened

   ○ to turn milk into cream and then into butter

   ○ to thicken milk into a creamy substance that is then chemically changed

3. What does the word "reward" refer to in paragraph 6?

   ○ the peculiar shaped dough that was baked by the monks

   ○ the children who were learning their prayers

   ○ the monks who invented pretzels

   ○ the money that was made selling pretzels

4. How do you think chef George was feeling when he accidently invented potato chips?

   ○ He was feeling happy.

   ○ He was feeling sad.

   ○ He was feeling angry.

   ○ He was feeling confused.

The History of Some Popular Foods: Questions

5. Which of the foods in the story do you think has the most interesting history? Explain your thinking and use specific details from the text to support your answer.

_____

_____

_____

_____

_____

_____

_____

_____

_____

_____

6. If you could invent a new food, what would it be? Describe what the food would be made of and how it would look and taste.

_____

_____

_____

_____

_____

_____

_____

_____

_____

_____

_____

SSG114   ISBN: 9781487704032 © On The Mark Press

Writing a Short Story

7. While taking a walk in the woods, you come across a broken branch, some feathers, and a nest with little eggs in it. Write a short story about the items that you found.

Ideas for my Story

_____

_____

_____

_____

_____

_____

_____

_____

_____

_____

_____

_____

_____

* Remember to check your grammar, spelling, and punctuation.

This page will not be scored.

Writing a Short Story

Write your story here.

_____

_____

_____

_____

_____

_____

_____

_____

_____

_____

_____

_____

_____

_____

_____

_____

_____

_____

_____

_____

_____

_____

_____

_____

SSG114   ISBN: 9781487704032 © On The Mark Press

Writing Multiple Choice

8. Choose the best order for the following sentences to create a paragraph.

    (1) But when people learned how kind Brigid was, they wanted to live near her.

    (2) At first, no one lived nearby.

    (3) A long time ago in Ireland there lived a young girl named Brigid.

    (4) Her home was a humble, thatched-roofed hut that she had built herself.

    ○ 1, 3, 4, 2

    ○ 3, 4, 2, 1

    ○ 4, 3, 1, 2

    ○ 2, 4, 3, 1

9. Which word is the plural possessive form of "woman"?

    ○ womens

    ○ womans

    ○ women's

    ○ woman's

10. Choose the pair of words that complete the following sentence correctly.

    _____, many people wondered where the miner got his gold _____ he never told anyone.

    ○ Later, since

    ○ Before, and

    ○ Because, but

    ○ When, because

11. Choose the word or words that are the best synonym for the underlined word in the following sentence.

    The judge <u>waived</u> the rule and the trial continued.

    ○ made

    ○ forgot

    ○ questioned

    ○ set aside

Early Aviators

The aviation industry would not have been able to move forward without the courageous and daring men and women who flew the planes. Aviators from the early and mid 20th century were willing to take huge risks to test the limits of aircraft design and to accomplish feats never tried before.

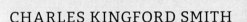

JOHN ALCOCK & ARTHUR BROWN

Brown (1886–1948) and Alcock (1892–1919) were British aviators who were th first to fly across the Atlantic nonstop. Alcock was the pilot and Brown was the navigator as they flew from Newfoundland to Ireland in 1919.

AMELIA EARHART

Earhart (1897–1937) was an American aviator and the first woman to fly solo across the Atlantic from Newfoundland to Wales in 1928. She and her navigator mysteriously disappeared in 1937 during an attempt to fly around the world.

CHARLES KINGFORD SMITH

Smith (1897–1935) was an Australian Pilot who made the first flight from the U.S. to Australia in 1928. He also made the first nonstop flight across Australia and the first flight from Australia to New Zealand.

CHARLES LINDBERGH

Lindbergh (1902–1974) was an American aviator who became famous for making the first non-stop solo flight across the Atlantic from New York to Paris in 1927 in his plane the *Spirit of St. Louis*.

AMY JOHNSON

Johnson (1903–1941) was a British Aviator who, in 1930, just two years after getting her pilot's license flew solo from England to Australia in 19 and a half days.

CHARLES "CHUCK" YEAGER

Yeager (1923–) was an American test pilot who flew during World War II. In 1947, he became the first person to fly faster than the speed of sound.

SSG114   ISBN: 9781487704032 © On The Mark Press

Early Aviators: Questions

1. What happened to Amelia Earhart in 1937?

   ○ She became the first woman to fly solo across the Atlantic.

   ○ She disappeared mysteriously during an attempt to fly around the world.

   ○ She became interested in learning how to fly.

   ○ She started her own aviation school.

2. Which early aviator lived into the 21st century?

   ○ Charles Lindbergh

   ○ Arthur Brown

   ○ Chuck Yeager

   ○ Charles Smith

3. Who were the first aviators to fly across the Atlantic nonstop.

   ○ Brown and Alcock

   ○ Smith and Johnson

   ○ Lindbergh and Yeager

   ○ Earhart and Lindbergh

4. What did Chuck Yeager do that no one else had done before?

   ○ He made the first flight from the U.S. to Australia.

   ○ He became the first test pilot to fly during World War II.

   ○ He became the first pilot to fly from England to Australia in less than 20 days.

   ○ He became the first person to fly faster than the speed of sound.

Early Aviators: Questions

5. Why do think it was important for these early aviators to take risks and test the limits of the aircraft of their time? Use information from the text and your own ideas to support your answer.

_____

_____

_____

_____

_____

_____

_____

_____

_____

6. Of all the things that these six early aviators did, which sounds like the most exciting and dangerous to you? Use information from the text and your own ideas to support your answer.

_____

_____

_____

_____

_____

_____

_____

_____

_____

SSG114   ISBN: 9781487704032 © On The Mark Press

Writing a Short Story

7. If you could be the first person to discover something, what would that be? Write a short story about being the first person to discover something that no one else has discovered yet. It could be discovering a cure for a disease, discovering a new type of plant or animal or a new kind of technology – anything your imagination can conceive.

Ideas for my Story

_____

_____

_____

_____

_____

_____

_____

_____

_____

_____

_____

_____

*Remember to check your spelling, grammar and punctuation.

This page will not be scored.

SSG114   ISBN: 9781487704032 © On The Mark Press

Writing a Short Story

Write your short story here.

_____

_____

_____

_____

_____

_____

_____

_____

_____

_____

_____

_____

_____

_____

_____

_____

_____

_____

_____

_____

SSG114   ISBN: 9781487704032 © On The Mark Press

Writing a Paragraph

8. Rewrite the paragraphs below using the correct spelling, grammar, capitalization, and punctuation.

Zach loves mexican food especially tacos enchiladas and nachos he decides to call some of his friends to see if theyd like to go out to dinner with him first he calls Miranda

hi Miranda said Zach would you like to go to dinner tonight I dont got Marks number will you call and see if he wants to go to

okay said Miranda im not doing nothing tonight ill call Mark and we can meet at the restaruarnt

Write your corrected paragraphs here.

_____

_____

_____

_____

_____

_____

_____

_____

_____

_____

_____

_____

Writing Multiple Choice

9. Choose the best closing sentence for the following paragraph.

   Tornadoes are among the most violent of storms in the world. They are responsible for the deaths of many people and millions of dollars in damage to property. Yet, they have also been known to do very gentle things.

   _____

   ○ Even writers have used tornadoes in their stories.

   ○ One tornado is said to have picked up a china cabinet and set it back down metres away without breaking a dish.

   ○ Tornadoes can pick up cars and trucks and completely destroy them.

   ○ Houses, schools, and businesses have been flattened by tornadoes.

10. What part of speech identifies the underlined word below?

    The old door <u>creaked</u> on its hinges and made a scary noise.

    ○ noun

    ○ adverb

    ○ adjective

    ○ verb

11. Choose the word that best completes the following sentence.

    Chocolate cake is the _____ tasting cake of all.

    ○ better

    ○ best

    ○ good

    ○ nicer

12. Which words are the best synonym for the underlined word in the following sentence?

    Jane noticed the bedroom door was <u>ajar</u>.

    ○ made of glass

    ○ tightly closed

    ○ partly closed

    ○ made in two sections

SSG114   ISBN: 9781487704032 © On The Mark Press

TEST #1: THE HIRED HAND

1. He thinks dogs are a waste of his hard-earned money.
2. an unattainable or fanciful hope or scheme
3. that they tend to be hyper and yappy
4. She suggests that Brady should do a little research.
5. good-natured and friendly
6. Irish terrier
7. small animals that cause trouble or harm to people
8. She wants to help Brady find a way to keep him.
9. be a good guard dog and protect the chickens
10. The henhouse was old and predators were getting in and killing the chickens.
11. Answers will vary.
12. Answers will vary.

TEST #2: A FRIENDLY LETTER

1. to ask for her help on a project
2. She lives in Peru.
3. the economy of the Americas
4. Summer
5. about 7 weeks
6. the way a country produces, distributes, and uses its money
7. Melanie is good at economics and math, her dad is an economist and they live in Peru.
8. Answers will vary.
9. Answers will vary.
10. maze
11. quicker
12. month
13. compound noun
14. bees are to honey
15. adverb
16. lessons
17. bldg.
18. prepositional phrase
19. amazement

TEST #3: DEALING WITH FAILURE

1. get something with great difficulty
2. his mother got very sick and died
3. It tells about his first failures.
4. He did not let setbacks keep him from pursuing his dream.
5. His son died at the age of four.
6. the American Civil War
7. It prepared him to deal successfully with hardship and adversity.
8. He set aside a day for the American people to give thanks together.
9. Answers will vary.
10. Answers will vary.
11. Answers will vary.
12. The Chinese are given credit for inventing the first real "nail polish."
13. quotation marks
14. kitties
15. "Haven't you finished the test, Troy?" the teacher asked.

TEST #4: FRESHWATER HABITATS

1. the amount of freshwater in the world's rivers, streams, lakes, ponds, and wetlands
2. rivers & streams
3. reeds
4. wetlands
5. frogs
6. Answers will vary.
7. Answers will vary.
8. Answers will vary.
9. 2, 4, 3, 1
10. verb phrase
11. Sentence 2
12. Before, still
13. Kids should soap up for as long as it takes to sing "Happy Birthday" twice.
14. were
15. lifted
16. Marsha's daughter will set the table; we'll cook dinner.

TEST #5: THE DOG AND THE SHADOW

1. Line 6
2. his shadow
3. to grab quickly.
4. He was greedy.
5. myth
6. line 21
7. The old-fashioned language and words like tittle, forsook and booty. Answers will vary.
8. It's better to be happy with what you have. Answers will vary.
9. Answers will vary.
10. Lions like to live in groups called prides.
11. plan the direction
12. Mars is to planet
13. likely
14. a. I don't want any ice cream.
    b. Teddy can't go anywhere for now.
    c. It really doesn't go any further.
    d. "I just love German chocolate cake," said Maria.
    e. Dr. J. Walley is now here.
    f. Marla doesn't want homework.
    g. I didn't do anything wrong.

TEST #6: THE CASTLE THAT LOVE BUILT

1. It tells about George's early years.
2. It was love at first sight!
3. He was intelligent and hard working.
4. St. Lawrence River
5. the fairy tale castle
6. They would use an underground passageway.
7. The Death of a Dream
8. George was going to present Louise with the fairy tale castle.
9. the process of becoming progressively worse
10. $1.00
11. He was heartbroken and didn't want to be there without Louise. Answers will vary.
12. It became a popular tourist attraction. Answers will vary.

13. Answers will vary.
14. Yes, Terry, there are thirty-one days in July.
15. The Andes are the world's longest chain of mountains.
16. more careful
17. 3, 1, 4, 2

TEST #7: LOCAL GIRL EARNS MEDAL FOR VOLUNTEERING

1. She had volunteered for three years at the Guide Dog Training Centre.
2. to explain what Michaela's job is as a volunteer
3. to move from side to side in an unsteady way
4. They stop the activity and pick up the puppy.
5. He thinks she is a perfect puppy trainer.
6. twice a month
7. returning the puppy to the centre when the puppy raising period is over
8. to officially be recognized as having specific qualifications
9. They begin formal training with guide dog instructors.
10. Answers will vary.
11. Answers will vary.
12. "What a gorgeous day!" exclaimed Melissa. "Do you want to go for a hike in the canyon? We can pack a lunch and take the dogs." "Sure," answered Keira. I'll bring sandwiches, cookies, trail mix, and water if you can bring treats for the dogs. It's 9:00 a. m. now; when would you like to leave?" "Let's see if we can be ready in an hour," said Melissa.
13. Sentence 3
14. Are
15. a smooth arc
16. Take an umbrella since unpredictable spring weather can start out sunny and suddenly turn to rain.
17. apostrophe
18. meal
19. adverb
20. Jonathan and Drew Scott are two ambitious Canadians who have made it big in the U.S

TEST #8: GRANDMA'S SECRET

1. forlorn
2. to a nursing home
3. to find a quiet place to grieve
4. not in good shape
5. She felt an aching need.
6. Grandma's first love
7. Gram's letters
8. shocked and surprised
9. when she is older
10. he died in the Great War
11. his brother
12. start
13. Answers will vary.
14. Answers will vary.
15. Answers will vary.

TEST #9: THE HISTORY OF SOME POPULAR FOODS

1. sandwiches
2. to thicken milk into a creamy substance that is then chemically changed
3. the peculiar shaped dough that was baked by the monks
4. He was feeling angry.
5. Answers will vary.
6. Answers will vary.
7. Answers will vary.
8. 3, 4, 2, 1
9. women's
10. Later, since
11. set aside

TEST #10: EARLY AVIATORS

1. She disappeared mysteriously during an attempt to fly around the world.
2. Chuck Yeager
3. Brown and Alcock
4. He became the first person to fly faster than the speed of sound.
5. Answers will vary.
6. Answers will vary.
7. Answers will vary.
8. Zach loves Mexican food, especially tacos, enchiladas, and nachos. He decides to call some of his friends to see if they'd like to go out to dinner with him. First, he calls Miranda.

"Hi Miranda," said Zach. "Would you like to go to dinner tonight? I don't have Mark's number. Will you call and see if he wants to go too?"

"Okay," said Miranda. "I'm not doing anything tonight. I'll call Mark and we can meet at the restaurant."
9. One tornado is said to have picked up a china cabinet and set it back down metres away without breaking a dish.
10. verb
11. best
12. partly closed

PHOTO CREDITS:

Page 51: Glynnis Jones / Shutterstock.com
Page 73: Alcock & Brown: Andrey Lobachev / Shutterstock.com
Kingsford Smith: rook76 / Shutterstock.com

SSG114   ISBN: 9781487704032 © On The Mark Press